Long Eye

LONG EYE

Kwoya Fagin Maples

HUB CITY PRESS
SPARTANBURG, SC

Executive Director, Publisher: Meg Reid
Managing Editor: Kate McMullen
Marketing Manager: Julie Jarema
Editor: Katherine Webb-Hehn

Book Design: Kate McMullen
Author Photo: Robert Farley
Cover art: Toshio Ebine

Type: Adobe Garamond Pro
Display: Karmasutra

Library of Congress Cataloging-in-Publication Data

Names: Maples, Kwoya Fagin,
1982- author
Title: Long eye / Kwoya Fagin Maples.
Description: Spartanburg, SC : Hub City Press, 2026.
Identifiers: LCCN 2025042322 (print)
LCCN 2025042323 (ebook)
ISBN 9798885740715 paperback
ISBN 9798885740722 epub
Subjects: LCGFT: Poetry
Classification:
LCC PS3613.A665 L66 2026 (print)
LCC PS3613.A665 (ebook)
LC record available at
https://lccn.loc.gov/2025042322
LC ebook record available at
https://lccn.loc.gov/2025042323

HUB CITY PRESS
153 N. Spring Street
Spartanburg, SC 29306
864.577.9349 | www.hubcity.org

"Our lives are a series of epic tales; we live and relive the odyssey"

—Hux Nichols

My husband's name is Marcus.
My daughters: Eden, Vivienne, and Maya.
I say their names because they exist.

Only 5% of the world's oceans have
been seen by humans.

Table of Contents

Prelude

Every body of water ripples in wind.
The sunball—tossed like salt onto waves—
sinks in beams that sound
beneath, clear to the living beds of varied corals
        whose chalices and tentacles drift in tide

Every morning the reef hosts its chorus:
in arrangements of clicks, burbles and whistles,
parrotfish crunching coral to excrete sand,
damselfish claiming thickets,
        while dolphins choreograph alluring displays

Every underwater being exists in relation:
eels and trout pair to hunt, the anemone
glamours to aid clownfish tucked in its flutter
and after its meal of sunlight, the reef
        feeds its own glaze of algae

Every animal being in concert
and I, why was I given this Atlantic body?
I bend the current,
refusing name or tether, seeking
        to be and move how I choose.

Blue Whale Chimera

Blue whale of capacious feeling,
many-faceted like grace.
When she is moved
beyond human griefs
she remains sustained
by an impossible love
at great depths beneath the sea

& maybe this explains
our fascination with wave,
how whole nights
wanting finds us restless
as docked boats, our
tangled sheets tied off elsewhere.

Too often we live on scarcity
while the blue whale plunges
below, simply grins to be fed
& her cheeks crowd with krill,
her satiation an afternoon
orgasm made since morning.

The blue whale hoards. Her heart
the size of a Volkswagen.
All the love we could want
down there in the dark.

When We Get to the Ocean I Don't See It

for the wonder of my daughters taking it in
collecting surf and sparks in three buckets
all lost in staying sure-heeled in gurgling sand
as if negotiation can be made
as if the water could be compliant

it is too early May for wading
still I rush familiarity, pull chilled waves
onto my thighs shivering
lie on the surface and swim
for the first time since my lessons

for all my wonder it is too early May,
my sharp yelps and gasping entertain my children,
who won't feel cold until they leave the water

minutes in, my limbs accept
My breasts and soft belly are last
clean is the word as I wrap arms around the sea,
even strokes and swift kicks

Attention Deficit Pastoral

Or how, if there is field before me—broad
sky and too much green—I lose my breath,
forgetting. Unable to keep up with my body,
now lifted off to wonder.
My children knock
around my knees, yet I can't hear their pulling.
So much is stunning me at once, the sun
on me at once. Why this?
I go in blind direction
smelling woods or earth or air,
so many roads of grass
under my shoes.

The Beach is Host to Small Things

Futile, like asking sun to show restraint
with my daughters' shoulders, the napes of their necks.
A nearby woman photographing her own precious things,
their small white feet kicking up the surf.
The man I love and my sun-lit girls skitter on the shore.
So much water to be gathered, collected in buckets.

Before the worst hurricane Charleston has ever seen,
my father showed us a kindness. Bringing us
supplies, then promptly leaving before the storm.
If his children were going to die, it wouldn't be
without flashlights.

As beautiful as the ocean day is in the morning,
I remind Marcus that morning sun is the worst.
The anxiety the sky reads today is racially motivated
incident. This sense of foreboding I sit with in predominately
white spaces. How this strained heart pushes past my sternum
to wrap the bright bodies of loved ones, pull them in.

The stupidest people in the world are police, my granddaddy said.
(In the '70s, my uncle went a few years impersonating
an officer, pulling folks over to write tickets and such.)
The man who fathered me always told me the world was mine.
Did a crab snap you? Vivienne asks.

Eden jumps over the waves how I did when I was a girl.
I will not tell my daughters to move out of the way
of the walkers on the beach this morning.

I will not hurry to adjust their positions for anyone.
I was born with a job to record.

Who does the sea belong to—
the man with the house on the beach?
Where is the plane and why didn't it deliver the message?
Is the ocean cold? I ask Marcus.
He says it is.

Autobiography of A Black Mermaid

All leave their boats in burnished skins, seal-slick
like picked stones skipped and slipping
to an Atlantic purse kept bulging with greed,
teeming with being

Though wilted or weathered, all speak
a kind of sweetness underbreath, morsels
of former lives mulled over and chewed down

Arrivals become a room of translucent rings of air.
Braids, waves and puffs stir the tide. Arrivals
inspire new expressions: bewilder-struck
or wonder-cast for what now expands the ribcage;
the school of winding fish that now swims the sightline

And they are all so long-eyed with wanting
it urges me. How to convince them?
There is mercy in water, relief,

for evil on land. By nature
they'll bemoan what's left behind
while thriving in this new home.

Should You Love A Poet

know i stay bun-naked, roll
beached in the sand of it;
the landscape a range of innumerable
castles i construct only to deface

a smudge of layered human musks
lend me unfamiliar & often
unknowable at the end of the day—
for all i bring to bed—

always a new oldness
compiling between us,
these strong arms
flecked with language
that crumbles sleep, the sheets
grainy with text dust

all day i work—escaped
figures & vowels underfoot,
residue lodged in work boots
i'll track to our bedroom

if you knew better you'd insist
i wear both uniform and gloves,
that i bathe long before lying down,
& hang my working clothes on a line,
cleansed in wind-bath all night

Another Severe Weather Warning

When I was a girl I dreamed of a boy
who climbed the forbidden fence to stab his father.

I was knife, somehow chosen to accompany
a gruesome stabbing that led to death.

Today, I am last to leave my hard seat at the patio table,
though sirens bloom, the rain

already speckling the page. Even the man
who's become my quiet competition rolls his magazine,

gives in, says, *the last time a tornado came through,*
it blew my roof off. I want to stay to watch the rain

break to pieces upon hitting the asphalt. I want
to take in the infant crying

murder from his stroller as his parents race
laughing towards their car, performing some romantic scene.

I like to peel polish off my nails like mica,
and I like to keep them painted the color of mica.

Sloan wore hers that way in *Ferris Bueller's Day Off.*
I think I wanted to be her pretty heart face, to kiss

Ferris Bueller fully inside the lips
before he jumped over the fence.

Things I am ignoring:
the pain in my right hand,

the pain in my right hip, my hair needing washing,
the creeping spider veins,

the girls on the other side of the glass,
the conversation about the rain,

the dog bowl left under the table,
the dog who won't die of thirst.

Things they are ignoring:
Another Black life swallowed by an old grief.

The first father gave me up. I was a slippy sea bass.
The thing crawling on his skin
microscopic, making his knuckle
itch, his grasp hungry for my mother's hair.

In spring, caterpillars infested the azaleas.
I've outlasted the tornado.

The Next-Door Neighbors, 1990

If we stood on top of the green generator in the backyard, we could see Marsha, bikinied, laid out on a lawn chair in the sun, turning from bread white to pink. White people love being naked outside, Dad said.

My mother never let us go to their house. If we played, Phillip had to come over (pale as milk and rat tailed) and he couldn't come in my room. And he didn't understand why we had to ask to get our bikes out, but we didn't understand how he could just take off on his, anytime.

There was one day, an afternoon where Phillip led us afraid past his mauve front door. I don't remember reaching Phillip's room—smell of pine combs making my head hurt—though I'm sure we did. I feel a tug now, on my wrist, pulling my brother and I back down the darkened hallway and out the front door, over the coarse grass and pine needles, back to the safety of our cracked driveway. Why should you care about this, reader? Are you even looking?

When we told Philip our parents were planning a garden, his dad suddenly built a wooden privacy fence on their side of the chain-link fence. We could see the heads of the sunflowers, soon after. Why did you tell them? My parents asked. I only had eyes for the pine tree roots in the grass. They were pleasing bumps under my bike tires. Can't say nothin' to white people, Dad said. They can't let you have nothin'.

Atlantic Origin

I gullah geechee people,
        open crab with my hands and teeth

I be sunflower seeds & boiled peanut shell;
        Rice every day, no bread

I be mali, nigeria, cameroon, or
congo—since by way of sullivan's island—
I be Black-trafficked

I be Granddaddy John and Grandmama Rose
        return from the Great Flight, so *Charleston*;
(I only wetdream child of eight-mile: its deadbeat)

At the market, I be sweetgrass baskets
        On the bay, Grandmama Rose washed floors;
I be Grandaddy cigar factory, I be paint on the Citadel walls

My people ate salt. Stayed on lots receding from Atlantic
as if by magic, (in truth, pushed back from the waterfront by greed)

Since they had the nerve to call marsh good foundation,
        I be whistling uncle, stacking your houses in the reeds

Thinning Sea-Bed of Clouds

A place to break through after meeting
The great mother, the sea, the womb from which
We all spring. If this is true and the seabirds
Skim the surface of the waves beneath,
Do we go to the clouds after the ocean
Swallows? Are we spat back down in rain?
Are we so many drops, dissipating in sand?

Seeds: the four boys that enter the sea in tandem,
Whipping their heads above the tide—
Even the beast of the sea is amused, giggles
Like a newly tolerant grandparent at their all-limbed
Leaps and hip tosses on the shore.

They've brought the beat with them—black speakers
On white shoulders—before standing in formation and
Moving in sync. We laugh, the sea and me
(The sea indulging us all) We all listen
As it roars for hours and yet we don't move an inch.

If I harness the siren, I call across the expanse
towards the tiny fish that make a meal.

I have furnished this Atlantic room with my own
hands, forever making, even this great
table of more-than-enough. They eat

until they flex and yawn, until the young invent
new games to pass time: trampling burrows
of funny fish who rise ruffled, scanning the depths

It's the sight of these creatures,
their potato-heads and mini-eyes, that arouses
the scene's *First-Laugh* and sends it

bubbling skyward,
signaling *home*

Folly Beach

My brother still bites his nails to the quick,
but lately he's allowed them to grow.
So much is forgotten with the horizon
as backdrop. It comes down to simple math.
The beach belongs to none of us, regardless
of color, or money. We all come to sit
at the feet of the surf, watch waves
drag the sand and crush shells for hours.
My brother's feet are coated in sparkly powder
that leaves a sticky residue when dry.
He's twenty-three,
still unaware of his value.
It is too easy, reader, for me to call him
beautiful, standing against the sky
in cherrywood skin and almond shaped eyes
in the sun. I tell him he is handsome instead.
I remind him of a day we came to the beach
when he was a boy. He almost followed a tourist,
a white man pointing towards his hotel—
all for a promised shark tooth. I yelled for him,
drove us home. Folly Beach. He was six.
He almost went.

((Quiet.))

My grandmother is/above the ground/and
beneath/my grandmother is in sky/blue curtains
her side/of the window/frame/a charcoal
portrait with/her/sister/*I told her she better*
not smile/sigh of laughter/last sign of life/before
/never to be/seen again/by outside/child
/smell of outside/my grandmother never sweat/nothing
/*wrong with a little*/*bleach water in your bath*/dear
form slipping the red dirt print/by rust picnic table/
it's not her/it's the shell/she's moved/to the sky/casket
/blue/dyed carnations/splayed/lying there/knowing
/I/carried a baby/to her death/bed/I'm having/another baby
/I said/could have/swore she chuckled past/nonverbal
of hospice/grated nuts pile in throat/
hold out/a slice of golden/apple on a gleam/of knife

Seeing You See Me

after RaMell Ross' photograph, "Shaquan"

as if we are here meeting eye to eye, consider
not assessing as I am infinite beads
past your abacus and you cannot know

this road or the soft business of my hands
or how the trees study sheltering
knowing joy is not merely transcendence

cause I don't think about european-americans
at any variation of Cookout
where the bass opens for Betty Wright to sing
a song even her own Mama told her not to sing
(on account of how free it is)

as if we could never be eye to eye, you keep watching
while you look like you smell like outside
you look like you been throwed away
you look just like a tinderbox dog with eyes big as saucers

not to mention, your head's so big it almost eclipsed my picture

what I'm trying to say is, I let my music breathe air, free to wander
while yours breathes like a slow-dying bass

this joy, a yellow brighter than sun
I hope you get something like it (some off-brand loop fruit not quite the same)

the light basks in my hair   and cannot be known
          like the truth   that my boot size is

a number,   the ground is damp enough to mark my tracks,
and you should really worry about   where I'm going

Once, I followed a dragonfish,
lured by its brave impetuous light.
Not a whisper could be seen in the moonless
dark; I lost my sense of down or up.
My arms weren't parting the frozen night.
Only baleens moaned across the plain,
startling my arctic abyss with life.

Now and then, a nudging curious mouth
woke the cuff of a shoulder, a fingertip
prickled

At last, a blur of scuttling sounds appeared:
in glow-white yeti crabs
squabbling over peaks of the ocean floor.
I settled in to watch,
making out lines of rock in the murky dark
until three eels further opened my sight

Was this when I began
breathing water with ease?

        Something
like a dress train, shifting
beyond my waist, revving up

And then, like the firefly squid
I could see again—precisely,
in full color

I could light up down to the tailfin,
                    glow red as a glass bird,
as a bloody belly comb jelly—I could see the way free

I Am Seagoing

boat set afloat,
She is mariner
          at the helm
My shoulders
she kneads
          like oars,
a motion coaxing
the smile into my lips.
          Face down
in darkness
I see now,
          the fjord of my breastbone;
          feel my belly—
always the whale shark—
opening
          and closing the water.
Because her hands:
a set of currents
          traverse my skin;
at last I breathe,
accept water through nostrils
lungs
swell like pleasure.
          I won't question my joy.
She doesn't question
the arc
          in my body
or offer the slack
diagnosis: *You've slept*

on your belly too long,
it's curved your spine.
She won't wring my spine
how that therapist did:
with pain—
as if it needed
Correcting, then—conceding
he'd *never*
seen a spine like mine.
But this sister
and her lemongrass oil
flooding the grove of my hairline—
I will be her boat, and
I do not care if we reach the shore.

Owed to the Atlantic

I began in you, spat you out once born.

You cover three-fourths of the earth
and own three-fourths of my body.

You grin, exuberant with truth. So easily
I could be in your belly, limbs

sprawled like an ocean spider,
recovered.

What was wind on land is current
What was wind-sound becomes reverb:
of tectonic crack, orca-scatter, Atlantic rivers
diverting saline lakes

What is wind on land is current,
What is wing on land is fin,

bird murmur: schooling fish,
tree grove: kelp forest

yet a valley is still a valley

Ocean is and we meld, all
undulate in assent

          Who could know
what the moon
is doing? Here,
time is measured
by tide.

The Proposal

seconds balanced in my palms—
            pin pricks, soft ticks
all at once
            your heart arrived, wearing
a leather bomber   to the minute

you'd ask me to marry you,

one jean knee on the sidewalk of Charleston's battery,
the same seawall
where I'd knotted cut lines to a reed   dangling
imagined fish

i've read that most of our conscious
            loving occurs alone, in the time we're apart
                        from our objects,
in linty pockets   of speculation

too often, what we imagine never arrives
but today,
we are us, blacklove
holding hands on Rainbow Row
pastel houses look on, tourists
watch from horse-drawn carriages
            while the Ashley meets the Cooper River

but how could i presume to know
the story underneath your coat?

i could only see myself
        on the opposite bank of the harbor:
it was low tide   and the day was clear

Oyster Meditation

You have yet to know the luck kept
in the bed of the oyster. Not the pearl, fool—
but the meat. Once pried, the top shell

tossed to the iridescent pile, pass all that remains
to an elder, watch an uncle or dad or mom carve
the steamy flesh up, and slurp oyster into
the dream-past of seen-it-all throats.
You are only a child.

What is left for you: shell-scrapes on the heel
of the hand that grasps it, a smell of the sea for days.
Oyster grit. Sediment. Algae mush in the seat
of flushed palms, start again. The job is to pick
an oyster from the oven pan shell-hot. Shift it
between your palms from relief to relief.

Again, you must find the catch in the oyster's body—
the way that will lead to an opening—all
with the underside of a butter knife grainy
with fossilized fragments. Loosen meat,
douse it in hot sauce—as if for your own
mouth, watering your mouth—
but pass it over to an elder. Tastebuds swell
in your jaws. You'll know this anticipation
better than the taste.

The Bee

It's a poisonous bee! Your stung-song panic.
I ran behind you, slogging in tequila sand
on honeymoon beach, *through sickness and*
in health on a loop.
When you asked me to marry you,
you asked me to forget what I knew,
What I'd seen of love—a home
on the back burner till it charred.
A mercurial affection, an itching to fight.
In light of it all,
you were still gearing up to ask.
I decided to marry you,
and I asked you to forget
your escapes to the woods on days
harder than my own.
I determined I would teach you,
I determined,
we would learn together.
And so, on our honeymoon
when the bee stung your ankle and you screamed,
I felt its poison shooting into my veins! I confess. It was me,
infecting you with all the hope I could muster.

The sound of gravel sinking under my tires, a steady crush of rock springing, sometimes pinging underneath my tires. We stop beneath an oak not oak, not sycamore but a tree old enough and dark enough to have been there for a while, though it has all its limbs and has accepted its wrinkles and the grooves grown in its bark. I explain this tree because it holds the moment. Where I don't look at my brother next to me on the passenger seat. It is the moment where I don't see him shift his secrets and fold them into his pockets like knives. It is the moment I don't ask why his young face looks as a weary as a grand-daddy. He is already shaking not shaking his head. We are already locked in the anger that I brought him here, before the wall of the tree before I ask and don't ask if he is on drugs. It could have been the moment the sky of my belly fell and an oyster shell hardened around my heart. If I keep writing this poem my brother will never seizure in the middle of Lowes. If I keep writing this poem he will rescind the admission that being altered is a lop-sided smile. I will bring him back from his far-away look.

Once, I lost something dear.

I would that the scales covered me wholly.
Porous, I am permeable, memory dissipates

All I magnified in a life before, now
formless, graspless as jellyfish pulsing, out of sight

When my pores are beyond holding
water, hair shrunken beyond its type,
the blue-whale arrives sea-celestial, her
          immense form overhead–her shadow
                    darkening the Atlantic room
The closer she moves I tense up,
rope scars and barnacle flecks on her skin,
one right luminous pupil, ever growing into mine.

          —

          I remember I am alive when my name is spoken:
she says I must be a mami wata, mother
          to the living sea and all its guests.
Her speech is dull and parabolic,
much is lost to competing sounds.

          I must maroon, gather, wait,
and not keep after my own thoughts

Once, I too, was caught
  by lure, the seize caress
    rendering me languid

Nature vs. Nurture

Months of trash talk over the phone so Dad was heated,
shoved the screen-door, crossed the porch til they stood nose to nose,

Ex-husband vs. New—Dad—sweat-lipped, ready-clenched, *You want me?*
My red father finding the smallest no in his square of the sidewalk.
He had only *wanted* my mother.

One of Dad's favorite stories is how he punked my father.

Put his head down, wouldn't even look at me!
And he better be glad he didn't!

In my adolescence, the story set me wondering
if there could have been more for me,
hidden that day behind my father's back.

Even though Dad had taken over the raising, there was
what came from Halbert Fagin. My freckled nose,
love of books, and eccentricity

The instinct to fight is harder to assign.

Unfold a Chair in the Front Yard of My Childhood Home

Outside in the light, I am socially distanced like a sun.

I gave my mom the universe this Christmas, its eight
planets and never-moon orbit her wrist.

We are waiting it out for our beloveds to grow
up, instead of down. There are angels heralding
on the windows, plastic bells beneath.

Such mocked depth is what I tend to.
I am lent to becoming an eyeball, tasting it all: pinetree
limp in boughs on the roof, copper strewn,
erratic combs

My mother always wanted
the pines cut down.

One did fly in a hurricane when I was too
young to light matches, couldn't strike right.

The staccato of Christmas pogo sticks to concrete—my daughters.
Sister, brother, mother, tucked inside the house.

Not everyone likes being watched
the way I watch. All these years,
the straw never fell while I was looking.
We are all here, but none of us are here.

I wasn't there when the angels were
hung against the glass. Only the sun
and the stop sign on Egret.

All the bouncing on the pogo sticks.
One daughter catches a gnat in her fist and then
sets it free on the calendar.

Three angels are lit, the others quiet.
A volley of leaps, the sunlight.
Vines growing up against the mortar.

Though you call and I come,
I am not your *Mami Wata.*

No *Sea-Mama; Yemaya*
Not your *La Sirene with baleen.*

I am a scarred angler fish,
hagfish!
Fear you haven't seen

Call me sea-beast-
salt-dredger, clay-slither
of last dreams

If I am the nightjar,
I will tear ocean–machete–
I will make like hurricanes who
unmoor ships and good sense

What *queen* deigns to traverse
a watery wilderness to collect stones,
to build homes for those railing against it?

          No. I may be
given to keep you, but not yours
No *Simbie*   No soul-guardian   No water-mother
If I were mother, I would not wean you
I would tear you from my breasts
I was only-once-I was   So once, I was
Now, I am   So I will be

Mom said we'd never had a beating. Extension cords had left her and her brothers bloody just for peeing the bed. & Granddaddy's dad had tied his sons by the wrists to the rafters of their shed. *It was a whipping*, she said. And I thought of the school library, its book, *The Whipping Boy*, though I knew Nijon was guilty of every act. Still, fury flooded me, made my hands fist, the left side of my head gleam with burn, striving to craft a forcefield for my brother, who gave me piggy-back rides if I let him suck on my cheek. I could watch him make parachutes for hours or stay to keep his head cool during fevers. I could share my cream soda and Slim Jim. But I couldn't go near if I heard him crying.

Passover for a Marriage

Rice & bean-smoke

was the season I went anointing,

smudging olive oil   to wooden entryways,

      making arcs over doorframes.

Covering,   the way   the Israelites

warded off
      their own angels of disaster   by blood   & hyssop

                  and with the same expectation

              I kneeled
rail thin on a Seventeen magazine (this before any stretch of hip)
      held up   olive oil in   petition

You see   my mother   had left the beans on   leaving
me an instruction   to watch and Dad, soon home from work

              So soon
kidney beans lima beans navy beans black eyed peas split pleas red beans
fifteen beans   northern beans   (& all with rice)   crust crisp
      and blackened
until my prayer was steeped in smoke.

I didn't know how to make
                the rice   they wanted
                the peace I wanted
            or any good of a steel pot of beans   left on high

These were days set   to unfurl in smoke   love would turn

                                                            hold to the angry pot

                                                                disavow   smack & pop
I want to call that girl up on the phone

            tell her the doorposts aren't hers   put the oil up on her own

Flash of Sister Shanna & Brother Jared

Inside, we imagine them *outside*. Sister Shanna and Brother Jared
synced-up behind our church building
rendezvousing Sunday nights, meeting every part
before their solos. They both sing. Nothing is lost to us.
They both have uncommonly   other-voices,   and we're hoping
Jared bites the butter: marries her, we and her hovering mother—though
he broke off his last entanglement.

We: thirteen, and still un-kissed working intently to inspect glimpses,
decipher the vowels of their whispers.
We capture it all, spread their secrets over our skin,   mouth their mouths
rounding over ours artfully in the dark.
Notes from the next track sound between them,
            and we make our way back towards the unforgiving light.

Once on a camping trip they'd chaperoned, I woke to Shanna in our tent, the moon of her white buns flashing as she bent over, her thong. She pulled her hiked dress down, then unzipped the opening of the tent, zip by zip, to sneak out and meet Jared.

Sister Shanna dies up   against a steering wheel. Leftover, the rich notes
of her voice,   a Pentecostal-puff, her fingertips pulling a dress over
a moon,   a lost *Oh*.

Soon After Dad Starts Going to Church With Mom the TV Set is on the Trash Heap

Its mute face appeared dead in the sun. If we watch tv at someone else's house, we will get in trouble. Half of us will do anything to not get in trouble. By ten, the best thing about visiting *granddaddyinthehospital* is the waiting room. It is where *nijonandkwoya* drink legal tv for hours, watching *National Geographic*, male lions brawling for prides, females taking down gazelles and tearing out taffy entrails—blood beards. Or boxing: where in corners men spill mouth guards, throw back their heads for streams of water, attendants taping and coaching even as the fighters leak and nod red, Don King's plumage just beyond the rope as they lurch back into the ring.

There are No More Lighthouse Keepers

a palindrome

on the way down
coiling
stairs after rainstorms
the tower grows
chilly, swaths of cloud converge
locking the watch room in gray

midstorm
the sky bowl appears
washed with guilt
punished
& wind whipped
sullen

in such constant shadow
the lightkeeper idled
elected to keep
after the lighthouse
(& yet unnoticing
too often beholding scenes
sunk in books
& a shame, those paid, rich eyes)
lost sea vessels in distress
so many unguided

sweeping land & sea in signal
keeping rounds
mated yellow birds
revolve up there now auto-

hypnotic the light left on
always

her own life
above the shoreline
moved as if ascending
forever, truths
dismissed
the last lightkeeper left,
useless as stolen whale-oil
forever burned out
on the way down

Even in this form, I can't disremember
a pleasing weight my collarbone and shoulder know,
an affection my mind can't scheme up

the blue whale is laboring.
Her movements bend, she
groans the enormity
Sometimes her eyes seek rescue
from the eyes of her surrounding pod.
Her sounds travel the atlantic room,
weaving whale bodies
and other species who wait quietly.

At last the newborn presents, slips out
tail-first, wrinkled and womb-shaped,
immediately precious, and vulnerable, and strong.
Somehow I expect it to turn,
Nose along its mother's skin towards
the leaking milk trail,
But she is whale, and first
it must learn to breathe

Nodding to its small body
the blue whale lifts the whale-pup
towards the surface
for its first spray under the clouds
—

Long after her sister whales and lingering guests,
past the songs
past wilting praise of her labor
I remain

I foil the orcas circling,
soothe her aches with kelp glaze, with stories
of the abyss—healing—

until her sounds are laughter, until
she plots for krill again
Sister, she says, pressing my face with her chin,
how do you know?—I am touching
her grey-blue skin, feeling below and around her fins

Only she discerns this innerheart, my feelings:
like bundled wood set on top a head before toppling

The nearby jellyfish keep opening umbrellas.
I answer only *I am not yours, I am free—*
The blue whale shifts
from my arms, leaves me with her tail to breach

The Plan

"Pay off the credit cards, pay off the car, buy a house, get the promotion,

It used to be a *BIG* secret, as in behind all
the doors of my slick mind

(the rented condo, bathroom vanity with ocean view
hands on the counter grasping a faucet

or whatever corner could be caught drunk
in pleasure tiptoe naked see my forehead

sometimes thud against the mirror
face left on the glass glance of the red

flush over my breasts) deep down
in hidden memory, yet,

thing is I was ovulating, had checked
the app, knew it was a prime day for becoming.

After, we lay in bed and a tiny star burned,
something like Keats's spark,

an impulse that led my hand
to find a nearby pillow, prop it—

as read sometime last year on the forum—
underneath my hips, stealthily

so as not to wake the would-be
father, who stirred, sleepily asked:

What Was I Doing? *Nothing,*
is all I said, before drifting off, *No-thing…*

but letting our babies begin their ascent
to my womb, take up room for two.

Nine Years Later We Ride an ATV Out in the Country

a worrying line between
your eyes, though the helmet holds my head—
still I could be hurt—leave you—
alone with our children,
and I pull on the warmth of this anxiety, a silk
robe fresh from the dryer and tied.

we straddle an ATV for the ride.
yellow dust and the rush-
blur of brick houses.
we can't hear anything for the blow
of honeysuckle air,
the engine of the four-wheeler rumbling.

we'd wanted to see it again:
the century-old clapboard church,
sinking where it will.
of course, we want to go in.
out here, there are no ordinances.
no one will come to condemn.

so we walk into the church holding hands.
poppy-colored lilies reach in
through broken window panes,
their leafy vines covering the sills.
was the floorboard broken by a shouting heel?

I tried to listen carefully to the preacher at our wedding.
I was listening too hard. I can only recall my sobriety.
over there was once an altar for prayer.

I drop your hand and move towards a piano with molded keys,
its pollen and mute hammers.
this is nothing new.
you've borrowed your father's boots.

we are here to witness disintegration,
crumbling pews and glass
shards of the old church.
I imagine how people attended:
every Sunday holy,
then one day not.

Expecting

More than anything, I craved my mother's bed. I wanted near her more than anyone else in the world. Her own mother died before she gave birth to her first child, leaving her longing,

but I had *her*. I indulged, unmindful of anything except my own comfort. When I felt labor pains in my body for the first time, I laughed. We'd taken five classes, all of them instructing us how to breathe. There was nothing that could have prepared me. I could only groan. I remember touching my belly after the babies came. The skin was dark, a sore plum. I felt stubble above the stitched incision. I started to count the staples, then stopped. The ones on the right end were tender. I was terrified of the day they'd be pulled. I didn't know yet I was numb and would continue to be, all along the line of the cut.

Sleep Deprived in the Waiting Room

I yawn when the babies yawn, eyes so burnt they can't sleep. We settle into hospital cushions, and I glance at my newborns,

peel away the blankets, so I can really take them in. Twins. Faces the color of acorns. A singular set drinking sleep. They arrived

premature, kept cased in the NICU for thirteen days, unable to nurse. This morning I dressed them against November and influenza, draped bright patterns over their seats. Quite suddenly, an owl alights in my periphery,

clicks from across the waiting room. I realize too late I've left them unsealed after my greedy check of their blossom faces. Prey. The owl is already cooing, curling gray feathers behind her ears. You know how new

babies smell. So the owl comes reaching, talons outstretched, poised to bestow upon baked infants her White Egg of Blessing. Me, frantic field mouse. Teetering on one-foot panic. Squeaking, "close the door, close the door!"

to their father, who is nearest to the exposed rose of our daughters' skin. Reluctant lion, he stands and smacks the owl's touch away, swatting the rings of her white reach

with his dark paw. In retreat, the owl is a wide-eyed frenzy. Baffled in her flight—to protection in any direction.

Love, Postpartum

An hour before, she'd pumped here
& in true form
shed the clutter of maternity ward

at the foot of our bed.
We gather mid-spread. Make out.
I kick at the flanges & tubes
looping my shins. Her milk coming
in as we kiss
makes it impossible to forget
our new address.
Minutes later

we hear a cry
we know must be met.
It's night, so we send him, the father
(like the book says to do)
bounding up the stairs.

Impossibly awake, I lay back
in the cushion of the dark room,
listening as our baby's cries are soothed
by a voice low and murmuring shushes.

You return now,
a suggestive pause in the doorway,
your silhouette easing off new fatherhood
like an evergreen shirt.
My breasts still hurt.
Self-possessed, you whisper

"what you'll do to me," all while
a forgotten glow-
in-the-dark
pacifier dangles at his lips,
muddling your seduction.

You, exhausted & unaware.
Me, engorged with laughter.

Shadow Monster

At last, I am larger and darker than life
and take up the space I ought to. I stride in new sunlight.
In this form, my charcoal fingers sweep grass on the median
across the street, a third knee grazes
a box of sweet tarts and flattens a sprig of flowering weeds.
I now carry four books instead of one.
We've almost reached the school where I teach,
though we stop to study
a wire shaped into a caged woman.
My new colleague ambles
absentmindedly in our direction.
We wait at the crosswalk, hold up a hand. His face hardens,
his bodyrecoils as if choreographed.
And though I offer a friendly tone, he is
stuck—engulfed, my shadows' heads looming
so far above his body!
His mouth slack,
eyes black-terrified,
of me.
We work together, I reach, shifting my bodies
out of the light, so he can see me.

Ms. Midriff

Only briefly flat sex snack, vanilla wafer cookie
Only once found worthy of naming,   (Peter)
                              & by then she was already
adulting, whispered to secretly
by someone who made us giggle.

This listless brain and belly date,
so she has hosted mini Milky Way family
reunions, Laffy Taffy graduations.
There could be twenty Riesens, or nine Tootsie
Rolls in ten minutes, a box of coffee Nips in one day.

She is giving bouncy house,
trampoline, finish line. (& this is just to name a few.)
She has always served herself, put herself first,
ahead of me without shame (& I find this most admirable.)

How the Atlantic Became an Influencer

Every body of water is stirred by wind. All waves
began with the Wave, first wave that circled the earth
        ~~giving wave~~
        ((and this is true))
that there is no end of ocean, that wavelets
rotate, meet us scrolling at the shore.

On wavelets, the sunball is crystallized sustenance,
((I regret this phrase))—let's say tossed
like salt on waves, its rays sounding the depths
clear to the sea kelp and corals to feed them.

Every morning the reef hosts a chorus of creatures, flash-
formation of clicks, burbles and whistles.
We don't often think of sounds beneath the sea—
        ((except for knocking billionaires'
lives we cry for, though amused at the memes, too—))

Still, parrotfish crunch coral to make sand. For tiny thickets,
damselfish come to fisticuffs, manifest destiny on the sea floor.

Even the dolphins choreograph lavish displays of self-care:
performative dance in the shallows.
Every underwater being exists in relation: Oh,
if we could exist in relation! Oh, word-lover!
If there was a place for heartfelt exclamation!

Every flora and fauna influencer generating content
has 100k more follow*ers* per follows.

On its reels, the anemone flutters its nude
BBL tentacles, ((glamourous subterfuge
for the clownfish tucked inside,
          and this is true.))
As part of its night-time skincare routine,
the reef feeds its glaze of hair algae.

I am just a mammal who can't tread or dive,
with low impressions @kwoyafagin.
There's still no brand for what I am or could be.

The Miracle of Us

Tennessee woman assaults man at Prattville hotel; stabs another at gas station
—WFSA 12 News + Staff, Dec. 2021

You wouldn't know *another.*
You wouldn't know I first nursed our children beside him,
nor how in one glance I noted
he held care for both
my wince and the infant need fastened,
its mouth the sting and quiver of a thrush.

Somewhere, at some time, your whole tongue
knotted itself to the bottom of your head.

Outside the sweat interior of your vehicle that morning,
gasoline fumes sent heads nodding into daze of scrolling,
fingertips to pockets to count change,
my love's back
magnetic as he picked up—
crayon debris, orange peels,

bubble gum wrappers from the floorboard.
There were your hands, too,
one winding hard on the vibrating wheel,
the other's thumb
stroking the teeth of a knife.

All this body has held his;
he doesn't belong to me.
I could never sign my name
to the known and unknown planet of his
body, I have not even

drawn a heart. And he has loved me
enough to leave me unmarked, no
dark sign of his visits
to this colony.

—the interbreath—

Praise to conspiring.
Praise for woven cotton strands and the work

of multi-hued hands gathering yards
from sewing machinery,
the brown eyes overseeing darting thread
that became

his shirt.

Praise the wind factor that urges him now, to slip on his suit coat too

and the breastplate all conspiring in protection,

the air:
a high of entropy and fury,

the curse of what brought you here knocking your unknown heart
and charged knife seeking anyone to open

and my beloved glows.

Praise. Both your
palm slip on the handle and unwieldy edge.

Praise synapse and startle, neurons that made quick journey
from the wound, spun him around to face you—blond blade

making access to a brown body,
weapon raised.

Praise be to YHWH, Nissi, breath
of all, that surged against the knife splitting
capillaries, vessels, dear undershirt, all work against the blade

Praise, Tennessee woman, that I was nowhere near to put my hands on you

& The Blue Whale Answered:

Let the sea ceiling be a mirror above us,
break and build a new home with its shards:

The only love to speak of is color
& The beauty to house is of color:

You are half-earth & I am the sea you know:
We both linger at what we perceive,
not understanding:

There are volcanoes in depths that could end me,
I've swum near the drifting smoke and its trench.
You are intent:

on claiming what could never be for long,
& striving to push off what's been purposed:

I am a large creature with small eyes:
Be a large creature with small eyes:

In the absence of light, navigate the ocean by ear,
sound travels faster beneath than above:
even when you aren't listening

Having only travelled over sea, my people are oblivious
to underwater terrain, to how it reflects land:
in seamounts, canyons, plateaus

They've never known the ocean is broader
than what they've seen of horizon

Though some recall betrayal, they'd return
as quickly as they sailed across
We trust you, mami wata, to take us home
What is home? I ask,
as their lie grows dense, eyes wide
to sightlessness

It's true. I could leave the scene I've made,
the home that never needed to be a palace,
just a solace for my people.
I could open and pull the water, east
towards an afterlife

With the African cliffs in view, I could tread
the intertidal
I am vigorous as the beluga,
but any closer I couldn't breathe
I could only point the way, imagine
a distant host of legs stumbling in surf,
waists wading the foaming shore

i.

Putting on her perfume nightly my grandmother would point to her temple and say—*what do the girl scouts say? Always be prepared?* and laugh into long breasts under her gown. She'd never given birth but raised five children. Her fingers wrapped round the bed post. She may have kissed me then, on the face, leaving a smell I couldn't wipe away. Her breath was old water. Only my little cousin Zynielle had the nerve to perfume our grandmother, crack open her closed casket and spray her Chanel #5, *every woman should have signature scent* just like she was getting ready for bed, for sleep in that powder blue casket, whereupon later we'd drop powder blue carnations: I'll always reach for flowers to drop in a grave. It was Zynielle held out the line to my paternal family, after. Reaching out, as I am an outside child, as I am wondering if my grandmother made Zynielle promise to IM chain memes of *Blessings* and glittering *I love yous.*

ii.

Maybe I offend the grave diggers when I offer *this is hard work*, as he and his partner lower the royal blue casket to the grave. It's fancy as a Cadillac—chrome alive in Mobile sun. I'd asked them to move aside the faux grass rug folded over my grandmother's headstone. I touched the bronze lettering and swelled, though I knew she wasn't there: *Oh death where is your sting*: When I speak, one man looks at me for the first time. The other had murmured *you alrights?* from time to time, as I stood there, lost by the ceremony of their work, as they took down the funeral tent, pole by pole, folded grass rug and stacked the flowers. The way they take their time lowering Zynielle's casket on taut belts into the grave next to my grandmother's makes me wish I would have spoken up at the funeral, and known her own favorite scent.

For Natylie

This card has a cheery codfish on its cover, and opening it reveals the words: *I got you this cod for your birthday.* And the card lacks weight and sentiment, a dollar or so, unlike its momentous and better sister—Hallmark—and maybe what the poet's sister actually deserved for her 29th birthday. Our mother has taught us to never count on a card to express sufficiently. There must always be words scrawled by hand underneath, extending what must be said. So this morning when signing I intended to write a heartfelt tribute at least a paragraph thick and without thinking wrote: *I love you more than a heart should.* And instantly knew it was true and there wasn't more to say, so I folded it, addressed it and sent it your way.

Elegy for Larry Freeman

How he took the world on, tender—
Like a sprig of gardenia blossom
pressed to his nostrils and inhaled
life as sweet as that,
like it all came back.

His laugh was a hungry laugh; his voice full-on
crooning his stories.
It could have been cotton in his voice box,
guitar against the wood panel.

He could really pick the good crabs, the oysters,
Season and cook them until your mouth watered.
And any homecoming or lucky Saturday
was always reason enough.
What could be wrong if we were eating crabs?

We'll remember he was always
there before he was needed,
His humorous bewildered looks,
And how even discouraged he seemed funny,
the movement of his dark hands, bright palms
Opening his stories, pressing together.

What he's left is record notes
to replay. His consistency and quiet love.
His sky blue and white truck pulling up in the yard, forever.
Him holding out a faultless gardenia for us to smell, too.

Blackberry Winter

We are all inside and the whole green world is out there.

False spring. Its only certainty,
stillness.

I keep ordering
things to open.

I am inside noticing all things missing

In my house—I can't abide—
this urgency only remedied

With a purchase to assuage
a grief, for not
Touching.

I am inside and the whole green world is out there, on Amazon.

Everything swells,
Does not brim over.

Until my mother breaks
At her end of the phone.

False spring, its particular
Want—everything and everything,

For nothing to be left

Missing: the rehearsal

Music for Tuesday's recital.
I become my daughter sulking in her leotard and tutu,

Thumb locked in her mouth.
It's a bad time for transitions, the article said—
I let her suck her thumb.

Ask my touch
how it knows human warmth more than
the slope of my own sternum,
how it goes where a heart first winced

This muscled fin enables me to carry ones
Struck, those who won't nest while the old scene
flashes on the black screen before them,
whatever locket face flickering

With time, my arms and interest fail,
I am queen.
        They whalefall, descending depths, lost to hagfish,
octopi, worms, until only bone mineral

        remains, littered on the ocean floor
I could mourn this, but I envy more
        their adornment—
whatever gilded thing kept them rapt in awe

And what is the story of their lives
between the seagulls? What is tossed
among them midair? What lines, gossip
for picking apart?

! The Looking War of Pisa !

reader, we wanted lunch before ascending the tower!
on sight! a european couple a table away launched!
their volley of tut-tutting eye rolls
towards my tribe! as we would only pervade
their illusion of ownership! even this
public garden café! even with
a whole table of space! between us!
they cherry-picked too close
for their upper lips! all set
in thinly disguised disdain!

i was compelled to use weapons on hand, yes! both eyes!
i turned my body (tourist and cannon)! their way
and made contact! which is to say,
i pelted them with unrelenting arrows!
staring! until one asked the other
about food on their face! gesturing eye-ward
in efforts to induce my shame!
somehow oppressors never prepare
for counterattack! but onwards! it's above me now!

while the drinks were served! & waiter re-arrivals,
through the salads! calamari and margherita pizza!
i met their every dart with mine!
and with a knell that proved quite fatal!
i smiled a fakest smile! (admittedly
of euro-american vintage!)

huffing huffs in finality! they set white flags on the table!
ended their white wine, and left!

Table for Black Family of Five in Firenze, Italy

i.

Ciao. Ciao. Ciao. Ciao. Ciao.
We greet the Eyes
as we are seated at our table in the square.
I guess we're on TV, Marcus says.
We have arrived for our shift,
I mumble towards the Europeans.
As if we've packed a movement,
A flock of European eyes swing in tumult.
Too many blatant hues of black—
five of us. Dinner is a series
of catching others capturing us, tittering
as we flounder with our nervous waiter,
our kids ordering America in Italy.
At the next table—front row—they
return a favor, ask if we want a photo after our dinner.
As if we need their flash on us, too.

ii.

Marcus settles on the train. Beside him,
a young Italian pulls his nose, runs a quick hand
through haircut, swivels for an alternate seat,
checks his watch, un-pockets his phone
glaring as I unravel the strap of my notebook.
Marcus signals me to ignore him.
We write too, I think. Escriviamo.
The man resigns, realizing we will remain.
Marcus opens his guidebook.
How does one keep a black husband safe
in any country?

iii.

morning-slice *Buongiorno*

slice
of cloth
breakfast
table

rented
light,

buongiorno

brown faces,
Venice plaits,

kiwi bite
held in grin

bonnets gold
cut
pineapple,
banana half-
collapsed

slice too
ray caught
between

shoulder
blades

cream-fern
coffee

just enough,
just us.

Autobiography of A Black Mermaid

Hot as a white-smoker, a sudden surge
sweeps the plain. We upwell, creatures caught
in a hurl of tidal current, carried swirling like marine snow.

Mid-breaker, the flounder whisper *jubilee*, the eels
easterly wind. We've been called to shore,
and I have learned against struggling.

We stream past the intertidal and into the marsh
archipelago. Through the waterways to shallows
where our heads emerge beneath a canopy of oaks.

When the wake stills, I rest on a mudflat of starfish.
The creek is moonlit around me, slick as looking glass.
My body is larger now. Skin the color of kola nuts,

Eyes glinting but indiscernible in the dark.
Though there is light on land, I luminesce. I preen.
Hip scales and fin-ray a red-flare display. My hair tangled

as oak drift. Here is my oil, here is my comb.
I will tend my plaits, make a nest of them.
I will wait quiet as a panther for what comes.

The air is sulphuric,
but there is no need to long
for deep water, or any place I am not.

Birthday

for Maya, Vivienne and Eden

A bus drove through my dream,
straight into the Atlantic
Wheels spun in sea floor,
in the undertow's suck and pull
the waves lap laughing
at rusted rims
salt waves swallowing   salt waves

~

You came—
by way of pink road   by way
of azalea blossom stain

So suddenly, you were here
hatched and shivering
eyes sealed shut in the passion
of arias,
red-faced and finger-splayed
like all the rest
        but mine

~

They held you up like bottles of wine,
pressed your cheeks against my lips
then whisked you off to cut our cords,
to cut my mermaid tale
and yours,
cut our way back to the sea
where we began, you and me

As If There is an Art to Losing

I gave you up before you left.
I'd already lessened the calls, caught

only in the new lives I was nursing.
The distancing

is the pulpy stone
beneath my heart, resting like a

blowfish in my ribcage.
I could never wait on what I knew

would inevitably come.
Like a first kiss,

I rushed your end. The last day
I saw you beeping and shifting

in a hospital bed, the nurse said,
Take as long as you want.

You mumbled you were cold and I
covered you, admitted
there was a new life in my belly.

I swore I heard you stifle a laugh, though they'd said
you were mostly gone, already.

I couldn't have stayed more than 15 minutes.
I was in something of a hurry to leave.

There was something in the golden apple slice
you offered one day, balanced at the end of your knife.
There was something in me not taking it.

Imagine seeing, upon waking,
a set of foot soles, like trout, flashing—
Igbo and Angolans
like strung beads as they spill
from a grounded boat, newly
made warriors, fighting captors in marshland
pummeling white faces red
Until one rises among them,
walks headstrong into the waves
and some follow,
fashioning their own deliverance
in reeds and water
—
I meet them at the bottom of the creek
Watching them, I chew the crayfish.
They will not meet my eyes as they feast.
They shudder as I press the bolus to their tongues.

They breathe *thank you, mama*, but only one
looks at me.

Black Heart

I have always been selfish and callous.

Since that photo, smiling from my daddy's hip,
my navel showing below a strawberry top—
his neck in the crook of my arm.

That's my daddy! I hissed in the Bi-Lo checkout line,
onto the cornrows of a little girl who dared
smile at him. Even then,
I knew I could be given up.

I have always been capable of stink.

Like a sailor, since five, my armpits
stun even me, and I've never gone more than a day
before washing them with hard hands.
Wound oblivious, I do things rough before I know.

My daddy said I was heavy-handed.

I'd creep. Cuff him on the sleepy fish skin of his back.
He'd laugh, stunned with the sting—
in awe of the ache of it—but when I bit him,
he bit me back, so I'd know the pain of it.

Three Heads of Hair to Comb

(((*Little bodies orbiting wherever I go*)))
People ask if I braid their hair.
I glance down hip-
level to the corn-rowed heads.
I am the corner they hang out on.
I flex my fingers still thrumming from the effort.
My fingers in *all that hair.*
I smile my answer and nod, and the stranger's eyes widen.
I don't know how you do it, they say, which annoys me.
What I want to say is:
My rat tail comb is a gleaming
Divider. The parts will be straight and thin,
Or curved, how I want them. Neat, because I am precise ((and you are not.))
It's all in the parting I say instead, like drawing.
You could do it too, if you wanted.
I draw up right behind the ear to the crown of their heads,
Apply oil, sealing ends, conditioner, and then take up
The smallest of three sections and begin
What I taught myself years ago,
Against a periwinkle sky in Iowa,
Before I ever carried a baby,
anywhere. I learned to braid at 23, while travelling.
In Iowa City, black people were scarce.
I braided myself past lonely, then
took it home.
I call it a "Round Robin" when I braid three heads: one girl after another;
in intervals so they can take breaks, get in the sun.
But not me. I go. I weave sections and let the girls pick the colors of their beads.
Seven beads on each braid, my back hot with pain.

My belly wanting for food,
but I want my daughters wholly loved.
They will be covered. Their heads are covered
with their mother's intention.

& what
does it mean
if you are set to think
like a viewfinder
and set to love like one, too?

& sometimes you can't
share a moon—
only you
can see it.

You alone saw future across the marsh
past the cypress grove

You alone saw the water as passage to home
You only missed that the water wanted all:

the bones and tiny hairs of your knees—
the slope of neck presenting
your finely made face, your eyes
placid despite the turbulence
of what brought you.

Yes, the water wanted you wholly,
any place I'd lay my head

Your broad nose crowns you Loango King
my voice names you, *Zow Uncola*

Before I can reach for you,
your face is to my waist again
Everything I love comes from you, you say
the words into my skin
Your voice a velvet horn:

We came by water, the water will take us home
We were stolen, we will not want for home,
we will away,
we will fly away

Wings open on your back, filling my hands
the force pulling you
to climb the tide with the others,
towards emergence,

Where above the water
You lead the murmur flying towards our African home.

You glide over the ocean that couldn't hold you
you navigate the air among the cranes and avocet

Below, I can hardly keep up, though my red tail whips foam
as if I could know salt from water

If I am revealed to you I am no goddess
For a time, I could be yours.

You can't hear me for the cry of the blue whale
breaching, her own heartbeat deafening
as she calls for her lost whale pup,
and I turn back for her

Invisible Work

or teachers guides whose gestures I recall better than names
so much I've been taught I have yet to know

but ode to every stitch of braid past my mother's fingertips
sewing countless
buttons for every day my grandmother
cooked and cleaned house twice

& Sis. Eugenia Foster
who kept my brother and me in summer taught me
steeping and drinking tea & how I could call for someone
but not cry when they passed over

the wind chimes too all their constant worry with wind

even after her stroke my grandmother Dorothy rose on cold nights
pulled a heavy leg down the hall
to cover me with a quilt
her own grandmother quilted

on his days off my only father
lacquered my found rocks
praised my keen eye
wasn't he urging me to notice?

I see now
all this gracious   lack of accounting   but maybe too
how tonight in terrific storm   when the wind picked up and pitched
warning   this primal body took off running
homing through the dark house
towards the beds where my children sleep

Postlude

If I am what is imagined I am washed up
on pebbled shore, sat melanin-sunning
on a stone in surf spray,
        all day primping with my pick and mirror

or I loaf on coasts to siren, posed little mermaid;
Intent on lending myself to be wanted,
so breasts cupped in shells, navel to sun,
        hip curve scintillating red,
through sunsets crooning
my longing for terra-form

If you could only see the grainy blues
of the intertidal: its urchin and sharks,
city-scape of coral, its channels of winding fish
        Or out further, in the midnight deep,
where lanternfish join other sea lights
studding the vast floor
you would know—

I do not forlorn, I do not long
        In this realm, where I've traced
the aching distance,
        solitude renders me
marvelous Atlantic body,
        everything in me warm
as the sunlit zone

Acknowledgements

Grateful acknowledgement to the literary journals and publications in which these poems previously appeared in various iterations.

"Invisible Work," *Academy of American Poets*, Poem a Day Series, February 2024.

"see you see me," In collaboration with the Ramell Ross exhibit: *Spell, Time, Practice, American, Body* (The Jule Collins Smith Museum of Fine Art and Southern Humanities Review), January 2023.

"Lightkeeper's Palindrome" *Gulf Coast: A Journal of Literature and Fine Arts* Print Issue 35.1, Winter/Spring 2023.

"Sleep-Deprived in the Waiting Room," *Gulf Coast: A Journal of Literature and Fine Arts* Print Issue 35.1, Winter/Spring 2023.

"Never Google How to Get Pregnant While Executing a Five-Year Plan," *Southampton Review*, Print Issue, Summer/Fall 2022.

"Sex After Baby," *Southampton Review* Print Issue Summer/Fall 2022.

"The Beach is Host to Dead Things" and "Here's an Ocean Tale," *Poetry Magazine*, June/July 2021.

"Nine Years Later We Visit a Church out in the Country" *Hypertext Magazine*, Spring/Summer 2021.

"Blackberry Winter" and "Shadow Monster" *#Being Counted Issue: The Thinking Republic*, October 2020. (Pushcart Prize Nominations, December 2020).

"The Proposal" and "On Finally Being Massaged by a Black Woman and Wherein we are Finally Ourselves," *The Langston Hughes Review*. Vol. 26 No. 1, Spring 2020.

"Attention Deficit Pastoral," *Tin House Review Online*, Fall 2019.

"Another Severe Weather Warning," "Sister Shanna and Brother Jared," and "Oyster Meditation" *Summerset Review*, Spring 2019.

HUB CITY PRESS | PUBLISHING *New & Extraordinary* VOICES FROM THE AMERICAN SOUTH

HUB CITY PRESS is a non-profit independent press in Spartanburg, SC that publishes well-crafted, high-quality works by new and established authors, with an emphasis on the Southern experience. We are committed to high-caliber novels, short stories, poetry, plays, memoir, and works emphasizing regional culture and history. We are particularly interested in books with a strong sense of place.

Hub City Press is an imprint of the non-profit Hub City Writers Project, founded in 1995 to foster a sense of community through the literary arts. Our metaphor of organization purposely looks backward to the nineteenth century when Spartanburg was known as the "hub city," a place where railroads converged and departed.

RECENT HUB CITY PRESS POETRY

black frag/ments • Lolita Stewart-White

the past is a jean jacket • Cloud Delfina Cardona

Lullaby for the Grieving • Ashley M. Jones

The Girl Who Became a Rabbit • Emilie Menzel

Joy is the Justice We Give Ourselves • J. Drew Lanham

The Last Saturday in America • Ray McManus

El Rey of Gold Teeth • Reyes Ramirez

In the Hands of the River • Lucien Darjeun Meadows

Thresh & Hold • Marlanda Dekine